The 20-Minute Bible Study Guide
Volume 1
26 Weeks
John, Romans, Ruth, Exodus 1-24, Hebrews
Psalms 1-48, 1 & 2 Thessalonians, Judges, Haggai, Revelation

J.A. Marucci

R.K. Brownrigg

INTRODUCTION

Congratulations on your decision to commit to studying the Bible!

This guide and workbook should prove fruitful in helping you grow. Here are a few tips to help with getting started and staying consistent. First, try to set aside a place with minimal distractions that you go to daily to read and answer the questions. Maybe it is a study, a bedroom, or a quiet place like a library. Generally, you will do better if you have a specific place where you go each day that has limited distractions.

Next, try to set aside the same time each day. If you are a morning person, try to do this first thing. Not everyone is a morning person, and many people prefer later in the day, evening, or during a lunch break. Whenever the best time of day is for you, try to set aside the same time daily. The guide is set up for Monday through Saturday use, and a day's reading and answering questions will usually take about 20 minutes.

Next, to get the most out of this guide, you will want to write down your answers to the questions. You can write in the workbook, as there is space under each question and a spare page at the end of each week's questions to write down notes. You generally will get more out of this guide if you write down your thoughts in response to the questions. If you don't want to write in the workbook, a separate paper notebook or digital document will work to record your answers.

Finally, it is normal to miss a time or two for various reasons. Don't let missing discourage you from picking it back up. If you do miss, or life gets in the way, just start again with today's reading, and move on. Try not to get tripped up because you missed.

Thank you again for taking this step to learn more about the Bible. All the best in your endeavor!

If you find this workbook helpful, please share it and consider posting a review on Amazon.

J.A. Marucci
R.K. Brownrigg

Name: _____ Date Started: _____

Weekly Checklist:

☐ Week 1 (Page 9) — John 1 – John 4:26
☐ Week 2 (Page 13) — John 4:27 – John 8
☐ Week 3 (Page 17) — John 9 – John 14
☐ Week 4 (Page 21) — John 15 – John 21
☐ Week 5 (Page 25) — Romans 1 – Romans 6
☐ Week 6 (Page 29) — Romans 7 – Romans 12
☐ Week 7 (Page 33) — Romans 13 – Ruth 4
☐ Week 8 (Page 37) — Exodus 1 – Exodus 6
☐ Week 9 (Page 41) — Exodus 7 – Exodus 12
☐ Week 10 (Page 45) — Exodus 13 – Exodus 18
☐ Week 11 (Page 49) — Exodus 19 – Exodus 24
☐ Week 12 (Page 53) — Hebrews 1 – Hebrews 6
☐ Week 13 (Page 57) — Hebrews 7 – Hebrews 13
☐ Week 14 (Page 61) — Psalm 1 – Psalm 18
☐ Week 15 (Page 65) — Psalm 19 – Psalm 29
☐ Week 16 (Page 69) — Psalm 30 – Psalm 37
☐ Week 17 (Page 73) — Psalm 38 – Psalm 48
☐ Week 18 (Page 77) — 1 Thessalonians 1 – 2 Thessalonians 3
☐ Week 19 (Page 81) — Judges 1 – Judges 6
☐ Week 20 (Page 85) — Judges 7 – Judges 12
☐ Week 21 (Page 89) — Judges 13 – Judges 18
☐ Week 22 (Page 93) — Judges 19 – Haggai 2
☐ Week 23 (Page 97) — Revelation 1 – Revelation 6
☐ Week 24 (Page 101) — Revelation 7 – Revelation 13:10
☐ Week 25 (Page 105) — Revelation 13:11 – Revelation 17
☐ Week 26 (Page 109) — Revelation 18 – Revelation 22

"...be attentive to my words; incline your ear to my sayings. Let them not escape from your sight; keep them within your heart. For they are life to those who find them, and healing to all their flesh." — Proverbs 4:20-22 (ESV)

Week 1 — This week's Bible reading will begin our walk through the gospel of John. We will look at Jesus the revealed Son of God, John the Baptist's testimony of Jesus, Jesus' first disciples, Jesus' first miracle, Jesus and Nicodemus, and Jesus and the woman at the well.

Memory Verse: John 3:18 — "Whoever believes in him is not condemned, but whoever does not believe is condemned already, because he has not believed in the name of the only Son of God." (ESV)

Monday
Read John 1:1–18

Focus on John 1:1–4. What do we learn about Jesus in the opening verses of this gospel?

What else are we told about Jesus? What are we told about those who received Him and believed in His name? (John 1:10–14)

What did John the Baptist say concerning Jesus? What other things are revealed to us in these verses? (John 1:15–18)

Tuesday
Read John 1:19–34

Focus on John 1:19–23. Who did John the Baptist say he was and was not when asked? What was his mission?

What did John the Baptist say when he saw Jesus coming to him? What are we told as to the reason for John's ministry to baptizing people? (John 1:29–31)

What else did John say concerning Jesus? (John 1:32–34)

Wednesday

Read John 1:35–51

Focus on John 1:35–42. How did Jesus' first two disciples begin to follow Him? What did Andrew do after spending the day with Jesus? What did Jesus say to Andrew's brother?

Who did Jesus call next to follow Him? Where was this man from? Who did Philip then find and what did he tell this person? What was Nathanael's reaction? (John 1:43–46)

Summarize the exchange between Jesus and Nathanael. Why did Nathanael proclaim that Jesus was the Son of God? How does Jesus respond to Nathanael's proclamation? (John 1:47–51)

Thursday

Read John 2

Focus on John 2:1–11. What were the circumstances of Jesus' first miracle? What was the effect of this miracle on His disciples?

What did Jesus find in the temple courts when He went up to Jerusalem for the Passover? What did Jesus do when He saw what was going on? What did He proclaim to those who were there? (John 2:12–16)

How did the Jews there respond to Jesus' actions in the temple courts? How did Jesus respond to them? What was Jesus doing in Jerusalem that caused many people to believe in Him? (John 2:18–24)

Friday

Read John 3

Focus on John 3:1–7. How was it that Nicodemus knew that Jesus was surely a teacher from God? Jesus uses the term "I tell you the truth" two times in these verses; what truths from Jesus should we be aware of here?

Why did God send His Son? What are we told about those who do and those who do not believe in Jesus? Why do certain people refuse to come into the light? (John 3:16–20)

Summarize what John the Baptist said here about Jesus. What does John say about those who believe in Jesus? What does he say about those who reject Jesus? (John 3:31–36)

Saturday

Read John 4:1–26

Focus on John 4:4–9. At what town did Jesus meet the woman who had come out to draw water? What are we told of Jesus' condition at this time? What did Jesus ask the woman and how did she respond?

What did Jesus tell the woman to do that opened the door for her sin to be revealed? How did she respond to this command? What did Jesus tell her about her past? How did she respond to His revealing her sin? (John 4:16–19)

Summarize the things that Jesus says in response the woman's attempt to turn the confrontation of her sin into a spiritual argument. What does Jesus say that makes it clear who He is? (John 4:20–26)

Study Notes & Weekly Highlights

Week 2 — This week's Bible reading will continue our walk through the gospel of John. We will look at Jesus in Samaria, the healing of the official's son, the healing of the paralyzed man, Jesus' authority to minister, Jesus as the bread from heaven, and Jesus teaching at the Feast of Tabernacles.

Memory Verse: John 7:38 — "Whoever believes in me, as the Scripture has said, 'Out of his heart will flow rivers of living water.'" (ESV)

Monday
Read John 4:27–54

Focus on John 4:34–36. In this passage, what did Jesus consider His food? What did Jesus tell His disciples about the harvest among them? To what sort of crop was He referring?

What happened in this Samaritan town because of Jesus' interaction with the woman at the well? After this event, who did the Samaritans believe Jesus to be? (John 4:39–42)

What was the setting of Jesus' healing of the royal official's son? How exactly did Jesus heal the official's boy? How did the official express faith in Jesus in this circumstance? (John 4:46–54)

Tuesday
Read John 5:1–18

Focus on John 5:1–5. What was the setting of this healing event? How many blind, lame and paralyzed were present at this place? What are we told about the man who Jesus singled out?

What did Jesus do when He saw the man who had been lying there? How did the invalid reply to Jesus' inquiry? How exactly did Jesus heal the man? (John 5:6–9a)

What else are we told about the timing of this healing event? Why did this bring persecution against Jesus? How did Jesus respond to the Jews in verse 17? (John 5:9b–18)

Wednesday

Read John 5:19–45

Focus on John 5:19–20. What do we learn here about how Jesus operated in ministry? What do we learn about the relationship between Jesus and His Father?

What do we learn about Jesus concerning His authority to judge men? What does He say about those who hear and believe in Him? What do we learn about the resurrection of the dead? (John 5:22–30)

What did Jesus say testified to His being sent by the Father? What warning can we take from verses 39–40? (John 5:36–40)

Thursday

Read John 6

Focus on John 6:1–13. Why did a large crowd of people follow Jesus to the far shore of the Sea of Galilee? How much food did the boy have that Andrew brought to Jesus? What exactly did Jesus do to perform this miracle? How many men ate, and how much food was left over?

How did Jesus define the work of God? How did the Jews react to this? (John 6:29–31)

Identify the word "bread" in this passage and list out what Jesus teaches in each instance. (John 6:32–58)

Friday

Read John 7

Focus on John 7:1–9. Why did Jesus purposefully stay away from Judea? Why did Jesus' brothers urge Him to go to Judea? What was Jesus' response to His brothers?

When did Jesus go to the temple courts and begin teaching? What was the reaction of the crowd to His teaching? What did Jesus say about His teaching? (John 7:14–17)

What did Jesus proclaim on the last and greatest day of the feast? What are we told that this meant? (John 7:37–39)

Saturday

Read John 8

Focus on John 8:12. Who did Jesus claim to be? What did he say about those who follow Him?

What warning did Jesus give those listening? What can we learn from this? (John 8:24)

What did Jesus say about those who hold to His teaching? What promise did He give to those who are His disciples? (John 8:31–32)

Study Notes & Weekly Highlights

Week 3 — This week's Bible reading will continue our walk through the gospel of John. We will look at the healing of the man born blind, Jesus the Good Shepherd, Jesus raising Lazarus from the dead, the triumphal entry, Jesus washing the disciple's feet, and Jesus as the only way to God.

Memory Verse: John 10:27–28 — "My sheep hear my voice, and I know them, and they follow me. I give them eternal life, and they will never perish, and no one will snatch them out of my hand." (ESV)

Monday

Read John 9

Focus on John 9:1–7. What did Jesus' disciples ask Him concerning the man who was born blind? How did Jesus answer their question? How did Jesus heal the man? What did the blind man do?

How did the man's neighbors respond to his healing? (John 9:8–9)

How did the Pharisees respond to the man's healing? (John 9:15–16, 28–29 & 34)

Tuesday

Read John 10

Focus on John 10:7–13. What does Jesus say about Himself in these verses? What does Jesus say about the hired hand?

What does Jesus say about His sheep and what He gives His sheep? What does He tell us about His Father? (John 10:27–30)

Why were the Jews about to stone Jesus? How did Jesus defend His claims of being God's Son? (John 10:33–38)

Wednesday

Read John 11

Focus on John 11:1–6. How did Jesus find out about Lazarus' sickness? What did He do in response to this news?

What was Lazarus' condition when Jesus arrived at Bethany? How did Martha respond to Jesus when she met Him? What did Jesus reveal about Himself in this exchange? (John 11:17–27)

How exactly did Jesus raise Lazarus from the dead? (John 11:38–44)

Thursday

Read John 12

Focus on John 12:9–11. Why did a large crowd of Jews go to where Jesus was? What was one of the results of Lazarus being raised from the dead?

How did Jesus enter Jerusalem? What was the reaction of those who came to meet Jesus? How did the Pharisees react to the people going out to meet Jesus? (John 12:12–19)

What does Jesus teach us about those who believe in Him? What does Jesus teach us about those who reject Him and do not accept His words? (John 12:44–50)

Friday

Read John 13

Focus on John 13:4–9 & 12–15. What did Jesus do in this passage? How did Peter react to this act of serving? Why did Jesus do this?

What are we told about Jesus identifying the one who would betray him? What happened to this person? (John 13:21–30)

What was the new command that Jesus gave us? What did He say would be the results of us obeying this command? (John 13:34–35)

Saturday

Read John 14

Focus on John 14:1–3. What did Jesus tell us to do in these verses? What information did He give us about the future place for those who trust in Him? What did Jesus say He would do?

What did Jesus say about Himself in this verse? What does he say about the way to God? (John 14:6)

What are we told about the ministry of the Holy Spirit? What name does Jesus use to describe Him? How would you define this name? (John 14:26)

Study Notes & Weekly Highlights

Week 4 — This week's Bible reading will conclude our walk through the gospel of John. We will look at Jesus as the vine, Jesus teaching about the Holy Spirit, Jesus praying, Jesus' arrest and crucifixion, and Jesus' resurrection and appearance to His disciples.

Memory Verse: John 17:3 — "And this is eternal life, that they know you, the only true God, and Jesus Christ whom you have sent." (ESV)

Monday

Read John 15

Focus on John 15:1–8. What do we learn in these verses about our ability to bear fruit?

What are we told is a key to remaining in God's love and having our joy be complete? What does Jesus define as the greatest act of love for others? (John 15:9–13)

From these verses what are we told we should expect from the world? Why are we told we would be treated this way by the world? (John 15:18–21)

Tuesday

Read John 16

Focus on John 16:7–11. What does Jesus teach here about the Holy Spirit and His work in the world?

What name does Jesus use for the Holy Spirit in this passage? What does Jesus say the Holy Spirit would do in our lives? (John 16:13–15)

Jesus uses the phrase "in that day" in verse 23. What day is He referring to? What does Jesus tell us about prayer in that day? (John 16:19–24)

Wednesday

Read John 17

Focus on John 17:1–3. Who was Jesus given authority over and by whom? How does Jesus define eternal life?

Why does Jesus pray that His disciples be protected? Why do you suppose this is so important? (John 17:11)

What does Jesus pray for those who would believe on Him through His disciple's message? Why does Jesus want those who believe in Him to be one? (John 17:20–23)

Thursday

Read John 18

Focus on John 18:2–11. Who led the detachment of soldiers and officials to arrest Jesus? Who drew his sword and cut off the high priest's servant's ear? How did Jesus react to this?

Who questioned Peter each time when he denied Christ? Where was Peter at these times? (John 18:15–18, 25–27)

Summarize Jesus' interaction with Pilate. What stands out to you in this conversation? (John 18:33–37)

Friday

Read John 19

Focus on John 19:1–3. How was Jesus treated by Pilate's soldiers?

How did the chief priests and officials react when they saw Jesus in a crown of thorns and a purple robe? How did the Jews justify their call for Jesus' death? How did Pilate react to this? (John 19:5–11)

What are we told about Jesus' death that ensures to the reader that Jesus did in fact die? How did His death fulfill prophecy? (John 19:31–37)

Saturday

Read John 20–21

Focus on John 20:10–29. How many different people did Jesus appear to after His death?

What are we told about other miracles that Jesus did? Why were the miracles in this gospel selected? (John 20:30–31)

What miracle did Jesus perform that opened the disciple's eyes to who it was? How did Peter react to the realization that it was Jesus on shore? What happened when they landed? (John 21:4–14)

Study Notes & Weekly Highlights

Week 5 — This week's Bible reading will begin our time in the book of Romans. We will be looking at the power of the gospel and man's condition, judgment and righteousness, justification by faith, the faith of Abraham, rejoicing in hope and suffering, and slavery to sin and righteousness.

Memory Verse: Romans 6:23 — "For the wages of sin is death, but the free gift of God is eternal life in Christ Jesus our Lord." (ESV)

Monday

Read Romans 1

Focus on Romans 1:16–20. What do we learn about the gospel in these verses? What do we learn about why men are without an excuse for believing?

What are we told about those who are mentioned in these verses? (Romans 1:21–27)

List out the characteristics noted of the people in these verses? (Romans 1:29–32)

Tuesday

Read Romans 2

Focus on Romans 2:1–4. Explain how we can condemn ourselves when judging another. What are we told about God's kindness?

What are we taught here about God's judgment and reward? What are we specifically told about God and favoritism? (Romans 2:6–11)

What do we learn here about inward circumcision versus an outward circumcision? (Romans 2:25–29)

Wednesday

Read Romans 3

Focus on Romans 3:9–12. What are we told about mankind's standing before God?

What is God's remedy for mankind's condition? (Romans 3:21–24)

What does it say that God did to atone for our sins? How is mankind justified before God? (Romans 3:25–28)

Thursday

Read Romans 4

Focus on Romans 4:4–8. What do we learn about faith and works as it relates to being made righteous before God?

How is circumcision defined here? Under what circumstances was Abraham given the sign of circumcision? Who is he proclaimed to be the father of? (Romans 4:9–12)

How is Abraham's faith described? (Romans 4:18–22)

Friday

Read Romans 5

Focus on Romans 5:1–2. What benefit are we told comes with being justified by faith? What hope do we now have?

What else are we told that we should rejoice in? Why are we told to do this? (Romans 5:3–5)

Contrast what Adam did with what Christ did. (Romans 5:15–19)

Saturday

Read Romans 6

Focus on Romans 6:3–7. What are we told about baptism in these verses? What does it say about our being united with Christ in His death? What are we to no longer be?

List out what we are told to do in these verses. (Romans 6:11–13)

Identify the words "slaves" and "slavery" in these verses. How are these words used in the context of sin and righteousness? (Romans 6:16–22)

Study Notes & Weekly Highlights

Week 6 — This week's Bible reading will continue our time in the book of Romans. We will be looking at the law, sin and the body, Israel and the stumbling stone, the process of salvation, Israel and election, and living sacrifices.

Memory Verse: Romans 12:21 — "Do not be overcome by evil, but overcome evil with good." (ESV)

Monday

Read Romans 7

Focus on Romans 7:1–6. How long does the law have authority over a person? What example is used to make this point? What specifically are we told about our old way and new way from verses 5–6?

What is Paul attempting to convey to the reader when he talks about not doing what he wants to do? (Romans 7:15–20)

What law does Paul speak of in these verses? Who did Paul look to for rescue from the condition he described? (Romans 7:21–25)

Tuesday

Read Romans 8

Focus on Romans 8:1–4. Why is there now no condemnation for those who are in Christ? How did God accomplish this?

How does Paul contrast life by the sinful nature and life by the Spirit? (Romans 8:5–8)

What are we told about things being able to separate us from the love of God? (Romans 8:35–39)

Wednesday

Read Romans 9

Focus on Romans 9:1–5. Why does Paul mention having sorrow and unceasing anguish of heart? What things does Paul say belong to the people of Israel?

Who are regarded as Abraham's offspring? (Romans 9:7–8)

What was the "stumbling stone" over which Paul said that Israel had stumbled? (Romans 9:30–33)

Thursday

Read Romans 10

Focus on Romans 10:1–4. What was Israel's critical mistake concerning God's righteousness? What are we told about Christ, the law, and God's righteousness?

How are we told salvation occurs in people? (Romans 10:9–12)

What is the progression Paul describes that enables people to be saved? Why is being sent by God so important to the process? (Romans 10:13–15)

Friday

Read Romans 11

Focus on Romans 11:11–15. What did Israel's transgression mean for the Gentiles and the world? What are we told Israel's rejection has meant? What will their acceptance mean?

What very sobering thoughts are we given in these verses? What are we warned to do and not do? (Romans 11:17–21)

Why has Israel partially been hardened, and when will this end? What are we told about Israel in verse 28–29? (Romans 11:25–29)

Saturday

Read Romans 12

Focus on Romans 12:1–2. What are we urged to do and why?

Examine the list of spiritual gifts. How is each one specifically to be exercised? (Romans 12:6–8)

Look at the list of instruction in these verses. Which ones stand out and why? (Romans 12:9–21)

Study Notes & Weekly Highlights

Week 7 — This week's Bible reading will conclude our time in the book of Romans. We will also study through the book of Ruth during the second half of the week. In Romans, we will look at the role of government, clean and unclean foods, and Paul's ministry. In Ruth, we will look at an amazing story of God's grace.

Memory Verse: Ruth 2:12 — "The LORD repay you for what you have done, and a full reward be given you by the LORD, the God of Israel, under whose wings you have come to take refuge!" (ESV)

Monday

Read Romans 13

Focus on Romans 13:1–7. Why are we told to submit to the governing authorities? What is mentioned about those who rebel against the established authority? What are we told about taxes?

What are we to continue to owe? What are we told sums up all the commandments? Why is this so? (Romans 13:8–10)

What are we told to do in these verses? (Romans 13:12–14)

Tuesday

Read Romans 14

Focus on Romans 14:1–3. What are we told to do in these verses?

What are we told about unclean food and how we should act around those who consider certain foods as unclean? How does Paul define the characteristics of the kingdom of God? (Romans 14:14–18)

What else are we told to do in these verses? (Romans 14:19–22)

Wednesday

Read Romans 15–16

Focus on Romans 15:4–6. What do we learn about the Scriptures in these verses? What blessing did Paul speak to the believers in Rome?

Explain Paul's mission and ambition as relayed to us in these verses? (Romans 15:17–20)

What warning were the believers given? What do we learn from Paul's final words to the believers in Rome? (Romans 16:17–18, 25–27)

Thursday

Read Ruth 1

Focus on Ruth 1:1–5. Why did Naomi and her family end up living in Moab? What happened to her family while in Moab?

How did Naomi try to persuade her daughters-in-law to stay in Moab? How did Orpah and Ruth each react to Naomi's urging? (Ruth 1:8–17)

How did the people of Bethlehem react to the arrival of Naomi and Ruth? How did Naomi explain her situation to the townspeople? (Ruth 1:19–21)

Friday

Read Ruth 2

Focus on 2:8–11. What did Boaz say to Ruth? How did she respond? What did Boaz explain as his reason for showing favor to Ruth?

How else did Boaz show favor toward Ruth? (Ruth 2:14–16)

How did Naomi react to hearing where Ruth had gleaned that day? What else do we learn about Boaz? (Ruth 2:19–22)

Saturday

Read Ruth 3–4

Focus on Ruth 3:1–6. What did Naomi tell Ruth to do and why? What did Ruth do?

What happened in the middle of the night at the threshing floor? What issue had to be resolved before Boaz could redeem and take Ruth as his wife? (Ruth 3:8–12)

What did Boaz tell the kinsman-redeemer initially and how did this man initially react? What else did Boaz say that caused the kinsman-redeemer to give up his right to redeem? What do we learn about Boaz and Ruth in verse 17? (Ruth 4:3–6, 13, 17)

Study Notes & Weekly Highlights

Week 8 — This week's Bible reading will begin a walk through the first twenty-four chapters of the book of Exodus. We will look at the oppression of the Israelites in Egypt, the birth of Moses, Moses fleeing to Midian, the burning bush, Moses' return to Egypt, bricks without straw, and the LORD's promise of deliverance.

Memory Verse: Exodus 1:12 — "But the more they were oppressed, the more they multiplied and the more they spread abroad. And the Egyptians were in dread of the people of Israel." (ESV)

Monday

Read Exodus 1

Focus on Exodus 1:6–10. What happened to the Israelites after Joseph and his generation died? What was the new king's attitude toward the Israelites? What reason did he present for oppressing the Israelites?

What happened to the Israelites as the oppression increased? How did the Egyptians react to this? (Exodus 1:11–14)

What did the king of Egypt command next? What did the Hebrew midwives do in response? How did God repay the midwives? (Exodus 1:15–21)

Tuesday

Read Exodus 2

Focus on Exodus 2:1–10. How did Pharaoh's daughter find the baby Moses? How did Moses get his name?

Why did Moses flee from Egypt to Midian? (Exodus 2:11–15)

What happened to Moses after coming to Midian? (Exodus 2:16–22)

Wednesday

Read Exodus 3

Focus on Exodus 3:7–10. What did God speak to Moses concerning the Israelites who were in Egypt? What do we learn about God's nature from this passage? What specifically did God tell Moses to do?

What was Moses' reaction to God's call on his life? How did God respond to Moses' reaction? (Exodus 3:11–12)

What did God tell Moses concerning the king of Egypt's response to his request to free the Israelites? What did God say about the Israelites' ultimate deliverance from Egypt? (Exodus 3:18–22)

Thursday

Read Exodus 4

Focus on Exodus 4:1–9. What three signs did God give Moses to perform before the people so that they would believe that God had appeared to him?

Why did the Lord's anger burn against Moses? What was God's solution to Moses' insecurity? (Exodus 4:10–16)

What happened when Aaron met Moses in the desert? What happened when Moses and Aaron met the elders of the Israelites? (Exodus 4:27–31)

Friday

Read Exodus 5

Focus on Exodus 5:1–9. How did Pharaoh first react to Moses and Aaron's request to let the Israelites go? What was the ultimate result of this first encounter with Pharaoh?

How did the Israelite foremen react to the decision by Pharaoh? How did Pharaoh respond to their plea? How did the foremen speak to Moses and Aaron concerning their situation? (Exodus 5:15–21)

What did Moses do after being confronted by the Israelite foremen? (Exodus 5:22–23)

Saturday

Read Exodus 6

Focus on Exodus 6:6–8. What specifically did God promise the Israelites He would do?

Why did the Israelites react to these promises from the LORD the way they did? (Exodus 6:9)

What did God tell Moses to do and why did Moses balk at this command? (Exodus 6:10–12)

Study Notes & Weekly Highlights

Week 9 — This week's Bible reading will continue our walk through the first twenty-four chapters of the book of Exodus. We will look at Moses and Aaron before Pharaoh, the plague of frogs, gnats, flies, livestock, hail, locusts, and darkness. We will also look at the final plague (of the firstborn), the Passover, the Exodus, and Passover regulations.

Memory Verse: Exodus 9:16 — "But for this purpose I have raised you up, to show you my power, so that my name may be proclaimed in all the earth." (ESV)

Monday

Read Exodus 7

Focus on Exodus 7:8–13. What did the LORD tell Moses and Aaron to do before Pharaoh? What happened as a result of this?

What things did God tell Moses to say to Pharaoh? (Exodus 7:15–18)

What happened when Aaron's staff struck the Nile? How did the magicians and Pharaoh respond to this? How did the Egyptians respond? (Exodus 7:20–24)

Tuesday

Read Exodus 8

Focus on Exodus 8:1–8, 12–15. What did Moses warn Pharaoh concerning? How did Pharaoh initially react to this plague? What are we told about what Pharaoh did after the frogs died?

What are we told about the plague of gnats that differs from the previous plagues? What is similar to the prior plagues? (Exodus 8:16–19)

What was different about the plague of flies compared to the prior plagues? How did Pharaoh initially respond to this plague? How did Pharaoh respond after the flies had left? (Exodus 8:22–25, 30–32)

Wednesday

Read Exodus 9

Focus on Exodus 9:1–7. What happened to the livestock of the Egyptians? What happened to the livestock of the Israelites? How did Pharaoh react to all this?

What do we learn about God's purpose in raising up Pharaoh? What warning was given to Pharaoh and his officials? How did they respond to this warning? (Exodus 9:16–21)

What happened when Moses stretched his staff out toward the sky? Where did it not hail? How did Pharaoh respond to this plague? (Exodus 9:23–28, 34–35)

Thursday

Read Exodus 10

Focus on Exodus 10:7–11. How did Pharaoh's officials react to the threat of the plague of locusts? What did Pharaoh say to Moses and Aaron? How did this conversation end?

What did Pharaoh do quickly after the locusts invaded the land? How did Moses respond to his plea? How did Pharaoh respond once the plague had passed? (Exodus 10:13–20)

What are we told about the plague of darkness and how Pharaoh reacted to it? What qualification did Pharaoh put on the Israelites leaving to worship the Lord? How did this interaction between Moses and Pharaoh end? (Exodus 10:22–29)

Friday

Read Exodus 11

Focus on Exodus 11:4–7. What were the specifics of this plague as spoken by Moses to Pharaoh?

What did Moses tell Pharaoh the results of this last plague would be? (Exodus 11:8)

What did God tell Moses to tell the people to do? How were the Israelites and Moses perceived by the Egyptians at this point? (Exodus 11:2–3)

Saturday

Read Exodus 12

Focus on Exodus 12:1–10, 29–30. What specific instruction did the LORD give Moses and Aaron concerning how the Israelites were to keep the Passover? What happened at midnight?

How did Pharaoh and his people react to this final plague? What did the Israelites take with them out of Egypt? (Exodus 12:31–36)

What regulations were placed on participating in the Passover? (Exodus 12:43–49)

Study Notes & Weekly Highlights

Week 10 — This week's Bible reading will continue our walk through the first twenty-four chapters of the book of Exodus. We will look at the Feast of Unleavened Bread, the Israelites crossing the Red Sea, the Song of Moses, the waters of Marah, manna, water from a rock, the defeat of the Amalekites, and the visit from Moses' father-in-law.

Memory Verse: Exodus 15:13 — "You have led in your steadfast love the people whom you have redeemed; you have guided them by your strength to your holy abode." (ESV)

Monday

Read Exodus 13

Focus on Exodus 13:3–8. Why did Moses tell the people to commemorate this day? How were they supposed to commemorate what the LORD had done for them? What were they supposed to tell their sons about this?

What do we learn about the consecration of the firstborn? (Exodus 13:11–16)

Why did God lead the Israelites through the desert and not through the land of the Philistines? Why did Moses take the bones of Joseph with him? How did the LORD's presence go with the Israelites? (Exodus 13:17–22)

Tuesday

Read Exodus 14

Focus on Exodus 14:5–9. What did Pharaoh and his official say after the Israelites departed? What does this tell us about their motivation to take actions? What did they do?

How did the Israelites react to the approaching Egyptian army? How did Moses respond to the people? What did the LORD tell Moses to do? (Exodus 14:10–16)

What happened after the Israelites crossed through the Red Sea? How did the Israelites respond to all this? (Exodus 14:26–28, 31)

Wednesday

Read Exodus 15

Focus on Exodus 15:1–5. What is the main theme of this song? What did Moses and the Israelites declare about the LORD?

What characteristics of the LORD are revealed to us in these verses? (Exodus 15:11–13)

What happened when the Israelites came to Desert of Shur? What did Moses do concerning the water? What did LORD decree to the people? (Exodus 15:22–26)

Thursday

Read Exodus 16

Focus on Exodus 16:1–5. What did the Israelites do after having come into the Desert of Sin? What instructions did the LORD give Moses for the people?

What happened that evening and the next morning? What did Moses tell the people to do? How did some respond to Moses' instructions and what were the results? (Exodus 16:13–16, 19–20)

What happened when the people saved the manna for the Sabbath day? What were the instructions for the Sabbath? (Exodus 16:23–30)

Friday

Read Exodus 17

Focus on Exodus 17:1–4. Why did the Israelites quarrel with Moses? What did Moses do in response?

What did the LORD tell Moses to do? How did Moses respond to the LORD? How did this place get named? (Exodus 17:5–7)

Who did Moses send to meet the Amalekites in battle? What part did Moses, Aaron, and Hur play in the battle? What was the outcome of the battle? (Exodus 17:8–13)

Saturday

Read Exodus 18

Focus on Exodus 18:13–18. What difficulty did Moses' father-in-law perceive when he watched what Moses was doing?

What role did Moses' father-in-law suggest for Moses? What solution did his father-in-law bring to the problem? What did he say the results would be? (Exodus 18:19–23)

How did Jethro, Moses' father-in-law, react to hearing about what the LORD did for Israel? (Exodus 18:9–12)

Study Notes & Weekly Highlights

Week 11 — This week's Bible reading will conclude our walk through the first twenty-four chapters of the book of Exodus. We will look at the Israelites at Mount Sinai, the Ten Commandments, laws concerning Hebrew servants, personal injuries and property rights, and the covenant confirmed.

Memory Verse: Exodus 20:12 — "Honor your father and your mother, that your days may be long in the land that the LORD your God is giving you." (ESV)

Monday

Read Exodus 19

Focus on Exodus 19:3–6. What did the LORD tell Moses when He called to him from the mountain? What promises were given by God?

What did the LORD say He would do and why? (Exodus 19:9)

What was the scene at the mountain on the morning of the third day? How did the people react to this? What did Moses do and how did God respond? (Exodus 19:16–19)

Tuesday

Read Exodus 20

Focus on Exodus 20:4–6. Examine the second commandment closely. What specifically did God tell them not to do? What is revealed about God's nature from these verses?

Look at the commandment to honor your father and mother. What promise is given for keeping this commandment? How is the final commandment different from the first nine commandments? (Exodus 20:12–17)

What commandment did the LORD reiterate with the people after giving the people the Ten Commandments? What instructions did the LORD provide concerning the altar? (Exodus 20:22–26)

Wednesday

Read Exodus 21

Focus on Exodus 21:1–6. What things do we learn about the treatment of Hebrew servants?

What acts resulted in the death penalty? When was the death penalty not to be enforced? (Exodus 21:12–17)

How are the phrases "eye for eye" and "tooth for tooth" used in context? (Exodus 21:22–25)

Thursday

Read Exodus 22

Focus on Exodus 22:1–5. What do we learn about the protection of property and penalties for stealing?

List out the commands stated here? What did the LORD specifically say concerning taking advantage of widows and orphans? (Exodus 22:16–24)

What other commands are stated in these verses? Which stands out to you and why? (Exodus 22:25–31)

Friday

Read Exodus 23

Focus on Exodus 23:1–9. What "do not" items are stated here? What do we learn about the treatment of the property of an enemy?

What instructions are given concerning the land during the seventh year? What reason is stated for resting from labor on the seventh day? (Exodus 23:10–12)

What did the Lord tell the Israelites to do when they reached the land where He was sending them? What benefits would their obedience reap? (Exodus 23:24–26)

Saturday

Read Exodus 24

Focus on Exodus 24:3–8. What did Moses tell the people and how did they respond? What did Moses do to confirm the covenant between God and the people?

Who went up the mountain and saw the God of Israel? What are we told that God did not do to these leaders? (Exodus 24:9–11)

Why did Moses go up the mountain? What happened when Moses went up the mountain? How did this appear to the Israelites? (Exodus 24:12–18)

Study Notes & Weekly Highlights

Week 12 — This week's Bible reading will begin our walk through the book of Hebrews. We will be looking at Jesus' position in the universe, His high-priesthood, Jesus and Moses, maturity and immaturity, and our hope.

Memory Verse: Hebrews 2:18 — "For because he himself has suffered when tempted, he is able to help those who are being tempted." (ESV)

Monday
Read Hebrews 1

Focus on Hebrews 1:1–4. List out what these verses tell us about Jesus, God's Son.

What are some of the things we are told about Jesus and angels in the scriptures quoted in this passage? (Hebrews 1:5–9)

What else are we told about Jesus in this passage? What are we told about the future of the earth and the heavens? What else are we told about the role of angels? (Hebrews 1:10–14)

Tuesday
Read Hebrews 2

Focus on Hebrews 2:1–4. Why are we told to pay more careful attention to what we've heard? How was our salvation announced and confirmed? Who testified to this and how?

What do we learn about Jesus? What do these verses say He did for us? (Hebrews 2:5–9)

What are we told the death of Jesus accomplished? What kind of high priest is Jesus? Why is Jesus able to help us when we are tempted? (Hebrews 2:14–18)

Wednesday

Read Hebrews 3

Focus on Hebrews 3:1–6. What is said about us as believers in this passage? What are we encouraged to do? What are we told about Jesus and Moses from these verses?

What are we warned about in this passage? What example is used here as a warning? (Hebrews 3:7–11)

Again, what are we warned about in these verses? What are we told to do for one another, how often, and why? (Hebrews 3:12–13)

Thursday

Read Hebrews 4

Focus on Hebrews 4:1–11. To whom did the gospel have no value? What are we told about those who believed the gospel? Why did some not enter God's rest? What are we told here about a Sabbath-rest?

What is said about the attributes of the word of God? What does it say God sees? What do we learn here about giving an account for our lives? (Hebrews 4:12–13)

What does this passage reveal about Jesus? What can we do confidently because of Jesus? (Hebrews 4:14–16)

Friday

Read Hebrews 5

Focus on Hebrews 5:1–6. What are we told about the role and characteristics of a high priest? How was Jesus made a high priest and in what order?

What insights are we given into Jesus' prayer life? What is said about Jesus' obedience and His suffering and what this brought about? (Hebrews 5:7–10)

What are some of the characteristics of immature believers mentioned here? How are mature believers defined? (Hebrews 5:11–14)

Saturday

Read Hebrews 6

Focus on Hebrews 6:1–3. What are the elementary teachings mentioned here that are said to be foundational? Which one of these teachings stand out to you and why?

What are we told about God and what He will do? What is said about how we show love to God? What are we encouraged to do in light of this? (Hebrews 6:10–12)

What do we learn about Abraham receiving what was promised? How are we told we can be greatly encouraged? What is said to be an anchor for our souls? (Hebrews 6:13–20)

Study Notes & Weekly Highlights

Week 13 — This week's Bible reading will conclude our walk through the book of Hebrews. We will be looking at Melchizedek, Jesus as our high priest, the earthly tabernacle, the power of the blood of Christ, the law and Christ's sacrifice, the heroes of the faith, and discipline.

Memory Verse: Hebrews 9:14 — "how much more will the blood of Christ, who through the eternal Spirit offered himself without blemish to God, purify our conscience from dead works to serve the living God." (ESV)

Monday

Read Hebrews 7

Focus on Hebrews 7:22–28. What do we learn about Jesus and His ministry as a priest?

Who was Melchizedek and what did he do? (Hebrews 7:1–10)

What is said about the power and longevity of Jesus' priesthood? What are we told about the former regulation and a better hope? (Hebrews 7:14–21)

Tuesday

Read Hebrews 8

Focus on Hebrews 8:1–6. What do we see concerning where Jesus is now and what He is doing? What are we told about the ministry of the high priest and the nature of Jesus' ministry?

What are we told in this passage about the old and new covenants? (Hebrews 8:7–9)

What major elements are we told about concerning the new covenant? (Hebrews 8:10–13)

Wednesday

Read Hebrews 9

Focus on Hebrews 9:1–10. List the elements of the earthly tabernacle. Who could enter the inner room of the tabernacle and how often? What was the Holy Spirit teaching us by this? When did these external regulations cease to apply?

What do we learn about what Jesus did and what He obtained? What does the blood of Christ do for us and enable us to do? (Hebrews 9:11–14)

What are we told that Christ did? What is every man's destiny? What do we learn about the nature of Christ's second coming? (Hebrews 9:23–28)

Thursday

Read Hebrews 10

Focus on Hebrews 10:1–4. How does this passage describe the law, its ability to cleanse worshippers, and its ability take away sins?

What is said in this passage about the power of Jesus' sacrifice? (Hebrews 10:8–14)

What are we encouraged to do in light of what Jesus has done for us? How can we put these instructions into practice? (Hebrews 10:19–25)

Friday

Read Hebrews 11

Focus on Hebrews 11:8–19. What things are we are told that Abraham did by faith? Which one stands out to you and why?

What do we learn about Moses from this passage and how he lived by faith? What did Moses consider of greater value than the treasures of Egypt and why? (Hebrews 11:23–28)

What are some other things the saints of old did by faith? How were some of them mistreated? Why were they willing to be mistreated? (Hebrews 11:32–40)

Saturday

Read Hebrews 12–13

Focus on Hebrews 12:4–11. List what this passage tells us about discipline. What are we specifically told concerning God's discipline? What are we told is the end result of discipline?

Concerning our relationships with others, what are we told to do? What are we told to keep our lives free from and why? (Hebrews 13:1–5)

What are we told to do concerning our leaders? What warning is given to leaders? (Hebrews 13:7, 17, 24)

Study Notes & Weekly Highlights

Week 14 — This week's Bible reading will begin with a four-week walk through the beginning of the book of Psalms. This week we will look at the blessed man, rejoicing in God, man's position in God's creation, the characteristics of the wicked man, the walk of the blameless, and the LORD as our helper.

Memory Verse: Psalm 4:8 — "In peace I will both lie down and sleep; for you alone, O LORD, make me dwell in safety." (ESV)

Monday
Read Psalm 1–4

Focus on Psalm 1:1–3. What characteristics does this psalm provide concerning the blessed man?

What trouble was David experiencing when he wrote this Psalm? What did he say concerning the LORD? What did he ask of the LORD? (Psalm 3)

What did David ask specifically of God? What did he rejoice about in the last two verses? (Psalm 4)

Tuesday
Read Psalm 5–7

Focus on Psalm 5. What are we told about God in verses 4–6? What are we told about the wicked in verse 9? What are those who take refuge in God told to do in verse 11?

What did David ask God for in this psalm? (Psalm 6)

What things are said about God in these verses? (Psalm 7:9–13)

Wednesday
Read Psalm 8–9

Focus on Psalm 8:3–8. What are we told about the moon and stars and the position of man in God's creation?

What did the David declare in these verses? (Psalm 9:1–2)

What is said about the LORD in these verses? (Psalm 9:7–10)

Thursday
Read Psalm 10–12

Focus on Psalm 10:1–11. What characteristics of wicked men does David provide in these verses?

What is said about the LORD? (Psalm 11:4–7)

What are the three main thoughts from these three verses? (Psalm 12:6–8)

Friday

Read Psalm 13–17

Focus on Psalm 15. What are the characteristics that David wrote of concerning those who may dwell in the LORD's sanctuary?

What did David say about the LORD and what He had done for him? (Psalm 16)

What things did David ask of the LORD? (Psalm 17:6–9, 13–14)

Saturday

Read Psalm 18

Focus on Psalm 18:6, 16–19. What are we told that the LORD did to help David?

What three things are we told in this one verse? (Psalm 18:30)

What things did David praise God for in these verses? (Psalm 18:46–50)

Study Notes & Weekly Highlights

Week 15 — This week's Bible reading will continue our walk through the beginning of the book of Psalms. This week we will look at the law of the Lᴏʀᴅ, dealing with feelings of being forsaken, the Lᴏʀᴅ as our Shepherd, how the Lᴏʀᴅ works among men, David's example, and David's plea for mercy.

Memory Verse: Psalm 27:1 — "The Lᴏʀᴅ is my light and my salvation; whom shall I fear? The Lᴏʀᴅ is the stronghold of my life; of whom shall I be afraid?" (ESV)

Monday

Read Psalm 19–21

Focus on Psalm 19:7–11. What are we told about the law, statutes, precepts, commands, fear, and ordinances of the Lᴏʀᴅ? What is said about these in verse 11?

What things did David desire for the reader? (Psalm 20:1–4)

According to David, what did the Lᴏʀᴅ do for him? (Psalm 21:1–6)

Tuesday

Read Psalm 22

Focus on Psalm 22:1–5. What experience was David relating to the reader? What did he declare about God in verses 3–5?

What did David say about God in these verses? What did he ask of God? (Psalm 22:9–11)

What else did David ask of the Lᴏʀᴅ? What did David say he would do? (Psalm 22:19–22)

Wednesday

Read Psalm 23–24

Focus on Psalm 23:1–4. Who did David say the LORD was to him? What did he say the LORD would do for him? Why was David not afraid of evil?

What are we told about the world in this passage? (Psalm 24:1–2)

Who are we told may ascend the hill of the LORD? What would such a person receive? (Psalm 24:3–5)

Thursday

Read Psalm 25

Focus on Psalm 25:2–7. What specific things did David ask the LORD for in these verses?

What did David say about the LORD's workings among men? (Psalm 25:8–9, 12, 14)

What else did David ask of the LORD? (Psalm 25:16–20)

Friday

Read Psalm 26–27

Focus on Psalm 26. Examine where the word "I" is used by David. What do we learn about him from this?

What was David's one request of the LORD? What was David confident about in verse 5? (Psalm 27:4–5)

In what else was David confident? What counsel did he end this Psalm with? (Psalm 27:13–14)

Saturday

Read Psalm 28–29

Focus on Psalm 28:1–2. What was David pleading for? What did he say would be the result of not hearing from the LORD? What was his posture in this regard?

What was David's response to knowing that he had been heard? (Psalm 28:6–7)

List the several things mentioned here about the voice of the LORD. (Psalm 29:3–9)

Study Notes & Weekly Highlights

Week 16 — This week's Bible reading will continue our walk through the beginning of the book of Psalms. This week we will look at David's petition of the LORD, David's confession of sin, precious promises from Psalm 34, David and his enemies, the love of God, and not fretting when the evil prosper.

Memory Verse: Psalm 34:18 — "The LORD is near to the brokenhearted and saves the crushed in spirit." (ESV)

Monday

Read Psalm 30–31

Focus on Psalm 30:1–7. What did David say that the LORD did for him? What are we told about God's anger and His favor?

What nine things did David ask for in these verses? (Psalm 31:1–5)

What do we learn about God's nature here? (Psalm 31:19–20)

Tuesday

Read Psalm 32–33

Focus on Psalm 32:1–5. Who did David say was blessed? What happened to David when he kept silent? What happened to him when he acknowledged his sin?

What did David encourage the righteous to do in verses 1–3? What do we learn about the LORD and His word? What are we told about how God created things? (Psalm 33:1–9)

What is written about being saved out of calamity? (Psalm 33:16–19)

Wednesday

Read Psalm 34

Focus on Psalm 34:17–19. What promises did David proclaim in these verses? Which stands out to you and why?

What are we encouraged to do? What promises are revealed here? (Psalm 34:8–9)

List out the four actions in this passage and the accompanying benefits from doing so. (Psalm 34:4–7)

Thursday

Read Psalm 35

Focus on Psalm 35:1–8. What did David ask God for in the first verse? What specific things did he ask God to do to those who sought to harm him (verses 4–8)?

How did David react to his enemies were sick? How did his enemies respond to him stumbling? (Psalm 35:12–16)

What else does David pray to God for in light of his enemies? (Psalm 35:22–26)

Friday

Read Psalm 36

Focus on Psalm 36:5–9. What do these verses teach us about the LORD's love, faithfulness, righteousness, and justice? What else do learn about the LORD?

What characteristics of the wicked are mentioned here? (Psalm 36:1–4)

What else did David ask God for? (Psalm 36:10–11)

Saturday

Read Psalm 37

Focus on Psalm 37:1–7. What are we told not to do concerning evil people and why? What are we told to do instead of fretting over evil people? What benefits are stated for doing so?

Find the word "wicked" in these verses and record what is mentioned in each case? (Psalm 37:12–21)

What do we learn about how the LORD deals with the righteous? (Psalm 37:39–40)

Study Notes & Weekly Highlights

Week 17 — This week's Bible reading will conclude our walk through the beginning of the book of Psalms. This week we will look at David's petition of God, the temporary nature of the life of man on earth, having hope when facing discouragement, our source of victory, and the reign of God.

Memory Verse: Psalm 46:1–2 — "God is our refuge and strength, a very present help in trouble. Therefore we will not fear though the earth gives way, though the mountains be moved into the heart of the sea" (ESV)

Monday

Read Psalm 38

Focus on Psalm 38:1–8. How did David describe his condition in these verses? To what did he attribute this?

What did David do while in this condition? (Psalm 38:15–18)

How did David conclude this Psalm? (Psalm 38:21–22)

Tuesday

Read Psalm 39–40

Focus on Psalm 39:4–6. What did David ask of the LORD? What is said about the life of a man and his pursuit of wealth?

What did David do and what did the LORD do for him? What did David say the result would be of God's work on his behalf? What are we told about the blessed man? (Psalm 40:1–4)

What did David say to proclaim to others? (Psalm 40:9–10)

Wednesday

Read Psalm 41–43

Focus on Psalm 41:1–3. What are we told about the person who has regard for the weak?

What did David's enemies do to him? What is said about his close friend? How did David reckon that the LORD was pleased with him? (Psalm 41:5–12)

How did the Psalmist encourage himself when downcast? (Psalm 42:5–6)

Thursday

Read Psalm 44

Focus on Psalm 44:1–8. What did God do for their fathers? How did they win the land? What else are we told concerning the victories that they experienced?

What was the present situation the Psalmist was describing? (Psalm 44:9–16)

What was the plea the Psalmist made to the LORD at the end of this Psalm? (Psalm 44:23–26)

Friday

Read Psalm 45–46

Focus on Psalm 45:6–7. What does the Psalmist reveal concerning God's throne and kingdom? What are we told that God loves? What does He hate?

What did the Psalmist proclaim about God and what was the result of knowing this truth? (Psalm 46:1–3)

What are we told about the LORD? (Psalm 46:8–11)

Saturday

Read Psalm 47–48

Focus on Psalm 47. What are we told about who the LORD is and what He has done?

What is said about the LORD and the city of God? (Psalm 48:1–3, 8)

What promise is stated here? (Psalm 48:14)

Study Notes & Weekly Highlights

Week 18 — This week's Bible reading will focus on the books of 1 & 2 Thessalonians. We will look at Paul's method of ministry, the resurrection of the dead, the signs of the second coming of Christ, and Paul's teaching on idleness.

Memory Verse: 1 Thessalonians 5:16–18 — "Rejoice always; pray without ceasing; give thanks in all circumstances; for this is the will of God in Christ Jesus for you." (ESV)

Monday

Read 1 Thessalonians 1

Focus on 1 Thessalonians 1:1–5. What were the things that Paul and his companions continually remembered before God concerning the Thessalonians? How did Paul and his companions know that God had chosen the Thessalonians?

What additional information are we given about the Thessalonian church? (1 Thessalonians 1:6–8)

What sign of repentance is mentioned here that testified to the Thessalonians' faith? What are we told Jesus will do for those who believe? (1 Thessalonians 1:9–10)

Tuesday

Read 1 Thessalonians 2

Focus on 1 Thessalonians 2:1–5. What was the general atmosphere in Thessalonica when Paul and his companions preached the gospel there? What qualities from Paul's ministry can be seen in this passage?

How did Paul and his companions minister to the Thessalonians? (1 Thessalonians 2:6–12)

How did the Thessalonians respond to the word of God? What happened to them because of this response? (1 Thessalonians 2:13–16)

Wednesday

Read 1 Thessalonians 3–4

Focus on 1 Thessalonians 4:2–8. What instructions does Paul give here by the authority of the Lord? What are we told about God's call on our lives?

What are we told to make our ambition and why? (1 Thessalonians 4:11–12)

What are we taught here about death, the second coming of Christ, and the resurrection of the dead? What are we told to do with these words? (1 Thessalonians 4:13–18)

Thursday

Read 1 Thessalonians 5

Focus on 1 Thessalonians 5:1–4. What do we learn here about the timing of the second coming of Christ?

Who are we as believers and what are we admonished to do in these verses? For what are we appointed? (1 Thessalonians 5:5–11)

Please list out the several instructions in these verses. Which stands out to you and why? (1 Thessalonians 5:12–22)

Friday

Read 2 Thessalonians 1–2

Focus on 2 Thessalonians 1:6–10. What do we learn about the timing of God paying back trouble to those who troubled the Thessalonians? What else do we learn about God's punishment?

Why did Paul write to the Thessalonians specifics about the timing of the Lord's second coming? What are we told must happen before the Lord returns and we are gathered to Him? What are the characteristics of the man of lawlessness? (2 Thessalonians 2:1–4)

How will this man of lawlessness be overthrown? What will be the evidence that identifies this man of lawlessness? Why are we told that people will perish by this deception? (2 Thessalonians 2:5–12)

Saturday

Read 2 Thessalonians 3

Focus on 2 Thessalonians 3:1–3. What does Paul ask the Thessalonians to pray? What does Paul tell the Thessalonians God would do for them?

What does Paul teach here about idleness? What example did Paul and his companions set for the Thessalonians? (2 Thessalonians 3:6–8)

Why did Paul and his companions not receive support from the Thessalonians? What rule did Paul give the church? What command did Paul give to those who were idle? (2 Thessalonians 3:9–12)

Study Notes & Weekly Highlights

Week 19 — This week's Bible reading will begin our walk through the book of Judges. We will look at the Israelite victories in Canaan, and also their forsaking the LORD, the first judges, Deborah's defeat of the Canaanites, the Song of Deborah, and the call of Gideon.

Memory Verse: Judges 5:8 — "When new gods were chosen, then war was in the gates. Was shield or spear to be seen among forty thousand in Israel?" (ESV)

Monday

Read Judges 1

Focus on Judges 1:4, 8–10, 17–19. What are we told of the exploits of the men of Judah — what peoples/cities did they conquer? What were they unable to do?

Who did Caleb give his daughter to in marriage and for what price? (Judges 1:12–13)

What do we learn about the exploits of the tribes of Manasseh, Ephraim, Zebulun, Asher, Naphtali, and Dan? (Judges 1:27–35)

Tuesday

Read Judges 2

Focus on Judges 2:10–15. What did Israel do after the time of Joshua and the elders who outlived him? What happened to them because of this?

What else do we learn about Israel and the judges God raised up during this period of history? (Judges 2:16–19)

What did the LORD say concerning the people violating the covenant given to their forefathers? (Judges 2:20–23)

Wednesday

Read Judges 3

Focus on Judges 3:5–6. What do we learn about the condition of the people of Israel at the time of the first judges?

Who was Israel subject to and why? What did they do in response to this? Who did the LORD use to save Israel and how did this occur? (Judges 3:7–11)

How long was Israel subject to Moab? Summarize how God used Ehud to deliver Israel from Moab? (Judges 3:12–30)

Thursday

Read Judges 4

Focus on Judges 4:1–3. What did Israel do after Ehud died? What were the results of their behavior? How did they respond to the oppression of the Canaanites?

Who was Deborah? What commands from the LORD did she give and to whom? (Judges 4:4–7)

What happened in the battle and who killed Sisera, the commander of the Canaanites? (Judges 4:14–21)

Friday

Read Judges 5

Focus on Judges 5:6–8. How does Deborah describe the condition of Israel when she became judge of the people? What are we told they suffered when they chose new gods?

What does this passage say about the involvement of the tribes of Zebulun, Issachar, Naphtali, Reuben, Dan, and Asher in the battle? (Judges 5:14–18)

What detail do we read about Jael's involvement in the death of Sisera? (Judges 5:24–27)

Saturday

Read Judges 6

Focus on Judges 6:1–6. Explain the condition of Israel at the time of Gideon. What did Israel do in response to this situation?

How did the angel greet Gideon? How did Gideon respond to the angel? What else did the LORD tell Gideon and how did he respond? (Judges 6:11–16)

What happened to Gideon and what did he do when the eastern peoples joined forces and crossed the Jordan? How did Gideon ask God to confirm that He would save Israel by Gideon's hand? (Judges 6:33–40)

Study Notes & Weekly Highlights

Week 20 — This week's Bible reading will continue our walk through the book of Judges. We will look at Gideon's defeat of the Midianites, Abimelech and Shechem, and Jephthah's leadership and rout of the Ammonites.

Memory Verse: Judges 10:16 — "So they put away the foreign gods from among them and served the Lord, and he became impatient over the misery of Israel." (ESV)

Monday

Read Judges 7

Focus on Judges 7:2–8. Why did the Lord tell Gideon that he had too many men for the upcoming battle? What did He have Gideon do to thin the ranks of the Israelite soldiers? How many went with Gideon into battle?

What did the Lord tell Gideon to do if he was afraid to attack the Midianites? How did Gideon respond to this instruction? What did he overhear that encouraged him? (Judges 7:9–14)

What happened to the camp of the Midianites when the 300 Israelite men sounded their trumpets and shouted? What specifically does it say that the Lord did? (Judges 7:20–22)

Tuesday

Read Judges 8

Focus on Judges 8:4–9. How did the men of Succoth and Peniel treat Gideon and his men when they were in pursuit of the Midianite kings? How did Gideon respond to each group of townsmen?

What did Gideon do to the elders of Succoth and to the town of Peniel in response to their not helping him? (Judges 8:13–17)

What did Gideon ask for from the men who had a share of the plunder of battle? What did he make out of this? How did it become a snare to Gideon and his family? (Judges 8:23–27)

Wednesday

Read Judges 9

Focus on Judges 9:3–6, 16–20. What did Abimelech do once the people of Shechem made him their leader? What curse was placed on Abimelech and Shechem?

What are we told happened after Abimelech had ruled for three years? Why are we told this happened? (Judges 9:22–24)

What became of the people and city of Shechem? How did Abimelech die? (Judges 9:42–49, 50–54)

Thursday

Read Judges 10

Focus on Judges 10:6–8. What are we told about the condition of Israel at the time of Jephthah? What was the outcome of their forsaking the LORD?

What did Israel do when they were in great distress due to being attacked by the Ammonites? (Judges 10:9–10)

How did the LORD respond to their crying out to Him? How did Israel respond to the LORD's rebuke? (Judges 10:11–16)

Friday

Read Judges 11

Focus on Judges 11:1–7. Who was Jephthah? Who called him back to be their commander? How did Jephthah initially respond to this?

What did Jephthah do to try and avoid a war with the Ammonites? How did the Ammonite king respond to Jephthah? How did Jephthah begin his response to the Ammonite king in response? (Judges 11:12–15)

What happened to Jephthah after the king of Ammon refused to respond to his claims? What are we told happened in the battle with the Ammonites? (Judges 11:29, 32–33)

Saturday

Read Judges 12

Focus on Judges 12:1–3. Why did the men of Ephraim call out their forces to fight against Jephthah? How did Jephthah respond to their threats?

What did Jephthah do to the men of Ephraim who had come out against him? How did this battle turn out? (Judges 12:4)

How were so many men of Ephraim killed in this battle by the men of Gilead? (Judges 12:5–6)

Study Notes & Weekly Highlights

Week 21 — This week's Bible reading will continue our walk through the book of Judges. We will look at Samson's birth, marriage and revenge on the Philistines, Samson and Delilah, and Samson's death. We will also look at Micah's Idols and Micah and the Danites.

Memory Verse: Judges 13:20 — "And when the flame went up toward heaven from the altar, the angel of the LORD went up in the flame of the altar. Now Manoah and his wife were watching, and they fell on their faces to the ground." (ESV)

Monday

Read Judges 13

Focus on Judges 13:1–5. What do we learn about the condition of Israel at the time of Samson's birth? What instructions did the angel of the LORD give to Samson's mother? What promises did the angel give?

What did Manoah pray for and how did the LORD answer him? What did the angel of the LORD tell Manoah and his wife? (Judges 13:8–14)

Why did Manoah fear for his life and what did his wife say to convince him that they were safe? (Judges 13:20–23)

Tuesday

Read Judges 14

Focus on Judges 14:1–4. Who did Samson choose to marry? How did his parents react to his choice? What else do we learn about this choice?

What happened as Samson approached the vineyards of Timnah? (Judges 14:5–6)

What was the riddle Samson told his thirty companions and the wager tied to the riddle? How was Samson's wife threatened concerning the riddle? How did she get Samson to tell her the riddle? (Judges 14:12–17)

Wednesday

Read Judges 15

Focus on Judges 15:1–6. Why did Samson take revenge on the Philistines? What did he do? What happened as a result of his actions?

What happened after the men of Judah tied Samson up to deliver him to the Philistines? (Judges 15:11–15)

What did the LORD do in response to Samson crying out to Him? (Judges 15:17–19)

Thursday

Read Judges 16

Focus on Judges 16:4–5. Who was Delilah and what did the Philistine rulers promise her in exchange for her getting Samson to reveal the secret to his great strength?

What three things did Samson falsely tell Delilah as to the secret of his great strength? How did Delilah finally get Samson to tell her the secret of his strength? (Judges 16:6–7, 10–11, 13–16)

How did Samson die? (Judges 16:28–30)

Friday

Read Judges 17

Focus on Judges 17:1–4. Who was Micah? What did he do with his mother's silver? What did she do when Micah returned it to her?

What else do we learn about Micah and the state of Israel at this time? (Judges 17:5–6)

Who came to Micah and what did Micah offer this person? What did this person decide in the matter? How did Micah perceive this decision? (Judges 17:7–13)

Saturday

Read Judges 18

Focus on Judges 18:1–6. Who discovered the young Levite priest on their journey? What did these men ask of the young Levite?

What happened when the six hundred men of Dan came to the house of Micah? How did the young Levite initially respond to the men taking Micah's carved image, the ephod, and the other household gods? (Judges 18:13–18)

Why did the young Levite priest change his mind and decide to go with the Danites? How did Micah respond to the loss of his priest and his idols? How did the Danites respond? (Judges 18:19–21, 29–31)

Study Notes & Weekly Highlights

Week 22 — This week's Bible reading will conclude our time in the book of Judges. We will also look at the book Haggai during the second half of the week. In Judges, we will look at the Levite and his concubine, the war with the Benjamites, and getting wives for the Benjamites.

Memory Verse: Haggai 1:9 — "'You looked for much, and behold, it came to little. And when you brought it home, I blew it away. Why? declares the LORD of hosts. Because of my house that lies in ruins, while each of you busies himself with his own house." (ESV)

Monday

Read Judges 19

Focus on Judges 19:1–3. What happened that brought the Levite to Bethlehem?

When the Levite, his servant, and his concubine finally left Bethlehem where did the servant propose that they spend the night? Why did they decide against this town? Where did they end up going? (Judges 19:10–15)

What happened to the Levite's concubine? What did the Levite do to show all Israel the wickedness of the men of Gibeah? (Judges 19:22, 25–30)

Tuesday

Read Judges 20:1–21

Focus on Judges 20:1–3, 8–11. How did the Israelites respond to receiving the pieces of the Levite's concubine? What did they resolve to do?

What message did the men of Israel send to the Benjamites? How did they react to this ultimatum? (Judges 20:12–16)

What did the Israelites do before they engaged the Benjamites in battle? How did the first battle turn out? (Judges 20:17–21)

Wednesday

Read Judges 20:22–48

Focus on Judges 20:22–25. What did the Israelites do after their first defeat at the hands of the Benjamites? What were they told to do? How did this second battle go?

After being defeated a second time, what did the Israelites do? What were they told to do? (Judges 20:26–28)

Summarize the events of the third battle with the Benjamites. Who won the battle and how many Benjamites were slain? What did Israel do to the people and towns of Benjamin? (Judges 20:29–35, 48)

Thursday

Read Judges 21

Focus on Judges 21:1–4. How did the Israelites react to defeating the tribe of Benjamin?

What did Israel do to secure wives for the 600 Benjamites who survived the war? Why was further action required? (Judges 21:6–14)

What plan was hatched to get the remaining Benjamites wives who had none? How did this plan work out? (Judges 21:19–23)

Friday

Read Haggai 1

Focus on Haggai 1:3–6. What question did the LORD ask the people through the prophet Haggai? What was the condition of the people in the eyes of the LORD?

What else did the LORD speak to them about their current condition and the reason for it? (Haggai 1:7–11)

What are we told about how the leaders and people responded to the word of the LORD through Haggai? (Haggai 1:12–15)

Saturday

Read Haggai 2

Focus on Haggai 2:6–9. What does the LORD speak to the leaders and to the remnant concerning what He will do? What is said about the glory of the present house versus the former house?

What does the LORD tell the people through Haggai regarding their past condition of lack and what will happen now that the foundation of the temple had been laid? (Haggai 2:15–19)

How does the LORD encourage Zerubbabel via Haggai? (Haggai 2:23)

Study Notes & Weekly Highlights

Week 23 — This week we will begin our journey through the book of Revelation. We will look at the resurrected Jesus, messages to the churches, the throne in heaven, Jesus the Lamb of God, and the six seals.

Memory Verse: Revelation 5:12 — "'Worthy is the Lamb, who was slain, to receive power and wealth and wisdom and might and honor and glory and blessing!'" (ESV)

Monday

Read Revelation 1

Focus on Revelation 1:4–7. What do we learn about Jesus and what He has done for us? What is said about His coming?

How does John describe Jesus' appearance? (Revelation 1:13–16)

What does Jesus say about Himself to John? (Revelation 1:17–18)

Tuesday

Read Revelation 2

Focus on Revelation 2:1–6. What did Jesus commend the church at Ephesus for? What did He hold against them? What did Jesus tell them they needed to do?

What did Jesus commend the church at Pergamum for? What did He have against them? What did Jesus tell them they needed to do? (Revelation 2:12–16)

What did Jesus commend the church at Thyatira for? What did He have against them? What did Jesus tell those to do who did not hold to the teaching of Jezebel? (Revelation 2:19–20, 24–25)

Wednesday

Read Revelation 3

Focus on Revelation 3:1–4. What did Jesus say concerning the church at Sardis? What did Jesus tell them they needed to do?

How did Jesus encourage the church at Philadelphia? What promise did He give this church? (Revelation 3:8–12)

What were the characteristics of the church at Laodicea? What was Jesus' opinion of their thinking they were rich and not needing a thing? How did He counsel this church? (Revelation 3:15–18)

Thursday

Read Revelation 4

Focus on Revelation 4:3–6a. How did John describe the One who sat on the throne in heaven? How did he describe the setting around the throne?

What were the four living creatures like? What did they do day and night? (Revelation 4:6b–8)

What did the elders do in response to the praise to God coming from the four living creatures? What were the specifics of the praise to God from the elders? (Revelation 4:9–11)

Friday

Read Revelation 5

Focus on Revelation 5:1–5. Why did John weep and weep? Why did the elder tell John not to weep?

Who did John see? What did the Lamb do? How did the four living creatures and the elders react to this? (Revelation 5:6–9a)

What are we told that Jesus did for us? What has He made us to be and do? (Revelation 5:9b–10)

Saturday

Read Revelation 6

Focus on Revelation 6:1–4. Describe the first and second horses and riders revealed at the opening of the first two seals.

What is depicted by the third horse and rider? What is the name of the rider of the fourth horse and what happens? (Revelation 6:5–8)

What did John see at the opening of the fifth seal? What do these ask God? What occurred at the opening of the sixth seal? (Revelation 6:9–10, 12–14)

Study Notes & Weekly Highlights

Week 24 — This week we will continue our journey through the book of Revelation. We will look at the great multitude, the seventh seal and the trumpets, the two witnesses, the woman and the dragon, and the beast from the sea.

Memory Verse: Revelation 12:11 — "And they have conquered him by the blood of the Lamb and by the word of their testimony, for they loved not their lives even unto death." (ESV)

Monday

Read Revelation 7

Focus on Revelation 7:9–10. How large was the great multitude before the Lamb? Where were they from? What did they cry out in a loud voice?

How did the angels, elders and four living creatures respond to the praise of the great multitude? (Revelation 7:11–12)

What else do we learn about this great multitude? (Revelation 7:13–17)

Tuesday

Read Revelation 8

Focus on Revelation 8:1–5. What happened at the opening of the seventh seal?

What are we told about what happened at the sounding of the first two trumpets? (Revelation 8:7–9)

What occurred at the sounding of the next two trumpets? (Revelation 8:10–12)

Wednesday

Read Revelation 9

Focus on Revelation 9:3–6. What type of creature was released at the sound of the fifth trumpet? What were they given power to do? What are we told men would seek at this time?

What happened when the sixth trumpet was sounded? What are we told about the horses and riders that John saw? (Revelation 9:13–19)

What are we told about the effects of the judgments on those not killed by them? What specific sins are mentioned? (Revelation 9:20–21)

Thursday

Read Revelation 10–11

Focus on Revelation 11:3–6. How long will the two witnesses prophesy? What will happen to anyone who tries to harm them? What are they given power to do?

What will happen to the two witnesses after they finish their testimony? Where will their bodies lie? How will people of the world react to their death and why? (Revelation 11:7–10)

What happened to the two prophets after three and a half days? What happened to the city at that time? (Revelation 11:11–13)

Friday

Read Revelation 12

Focus on Revelation 12:1–6. What are some things we learn about the woman and the dragon from these verses?

Who do we learn is the ancient dragon? What does it say he did day and night before God prior to being hurled down to the earth? How did they overcome the dragon? (Revelation 12:9–11)

What does it say the dragon did after being enraged at the woman who escaped his grasp? (Revelation 12:15–17)

Saturday

Read Revelation 13:1–10

Focus on Revelation 13:1–4. What are the characteristics of the beast that came out of the sea? What does it say happened to one of the heads of the beast? How did the world react to this?

How long does the beast exercise authority and blaspheme for, and who does he slander? Who does he conquer and who is he given power over? (Revelation 13:5–7)

Who worships the beast? What warning is given to the saints of this time? (Revelation 13:8–10)

Study Notes & Weekly Highlights

Week 25 — This week we will continue our journey through the book of Revelation. We will look at the beast out of the earth, the 144,000 and the three angels, the two harvests, the seven bowls of final judgment, and the woman on the beast.

Memory Verse: Revelation 15:3b — "Great and amazing are your deeds, O Lord God the Almighty! Just and true are your ways, O King of the nations!" (ESV)

Monday

Read Revelation 13:11–18

Focus on Revelation 13:11–12. How is this beast described? What authority does he exercise? What does he make the inhabitants of the earth do?

How does this beast deceive the inhabitants of the earth? What more do we learn about the first beast in these verses? (Revelation 13:13–14)

What else does the second beast do? What are we told is the number of the first beast's name? (Revelation 13:14b–18)

Tuesday

Read Revelation 14:1–11

Focus on Revelation 14:1–5. What are we told about the 144,000?

What did the first two angels proclaim to those alive on the earth? (Revelation 14:6–8)

Summarize the third angel's proclamation. (Revelation 14:9–11)

Wednesday

Read Revelation 14:12–20

Focus on Revelation 14:14–16. Who was seated on the white cloud? What did He have in His hand? What does He do?

What does each of the angels in this passage do? (Revelation 14:17–19)

What are we told happens to those of the earth gathered for the winepress of God's wrath? (Revelation 14:20)

Thursday

Read Revelation 15–16:7

Focus on Revelation 15:2–4. Who is seen standing beside the sea that looked like glass and fire? What are they given and what song do they sing?

What happens when the first two angels pour out their bowls of God's wrath on the earth? (Revelation 16:1–3)

What happens when the third angel pours out his bowl? What reaction does the angel in charge of the waters say in response to this? (Revelation 16:4–7)

Friday

Read Revelation 16:8–21

Focus on Revelation 16:8–11. What happens when the fourth and fifth bowls of God's wrath are poured out? What is said in both cases regarding man's response?

What does the sixth bowl being poured out bring about? What are we told in verse 15? (Revelation 16:12–16)

Summarize what happens when the seventh and final bowl of judgment is poured out. (Revelation 16:17–21)

Saturday

Read Revelation 17

Focus on Revelation 17:3–6. How is the woman on the scarlet beast described? What was the title on her forehead? What was she drunk with?

Who will be astonished by the beast? Why will they be astonished? (Revelation 17:8)

What do we learn about the ten horns, their purpose, and their end? (Revelation 17:12–14)

Study Notes & Weekly Highlights

Week 26 — This week we will conclude our journey through the book of Revelation. We will look at the fall of Babylon, the rider on the white horse, the thousand-year reign, the judgments, the new Jerusalem, and Jesus' reward.

Memory Verse: Revelation 22:12 — "Behold, I am coming soon, bringing my recompense with me, to repay each one for what he has done." (ESV)

Monday

Read Revelation 18

Focus on Revelation 18:1–3. What are we told about Babylon the Great?

How do the merchants react to the fall of Babylon? (Revelation 18:11–17)

Who is told to rejoice over Babylon's destruction and why? What things are said to never happen in Babylon after her destruction? What is to be found in this city concerning the prophets and saints? (Revelation 18:20–24)

Tuesday

Read Revelation 19

Focus on Revelation 19:11–13. What are we told about the rider on the white horse?

Who was following the rider on the white horse? What else are we told about the rider? (Revelation 19:14–16)

Who are the opponents in this war? What are we told happens to the beast and the false prophet? What happens to the rest of the armies? (Revelation 19:19–21)

Wednesday

Read Revelation 20:1–6

Focus on Revelation 20:1–3. What are we told will happen to Satan at this time? Who will accomplish this? What are we told he will not be able to do during this thousand-year period?

What does this verse tell us? (Revelation 20:4)

When are we told the rest of the dead would come to life? What happens to those who are part of this first resurrection? (Revelation 20:5–6)

Thursday

Read Revelation 20:7–15

Focus on Revelation 20:7–10. What does Satan do after his release from prison? What happens to the devil and those who follow him?

What happens when God appears seated on His great white throne? How are we told the dead will be judged? (Revelation 20:11–12)

How are we told each person in this judgment will be judged? What are we told will be the end of those whose names are not found written in the book of life? (Revelation 20:13–15)

Friday

Read Revelation 21

Focus on Revelation 21:1–4. What do we learn about the new Jerusalem? What else do we learn concerning the new state of things from the loud voice from the throne?

What promises from Jesus are given in verses 6 and 7? Who are we told will have their place in the lake of fire? (Revelation 21:6–8)

How large is the city — the new Jerusalem? How thick are its walls? (Revelation 21:15–17)

Saturday

Read Revelation 22

Focus on Revelation 22:1–5. List out the characteristics of the city and the future state given here.

What does Jesus say about His reward? What does this passage say gives one the right to the tree of life and to go through the gates into the city? Who is left outside? (Revelation 22:12–15)

What warnings are given to those who would alter the words of this book? (Revelation 22:18–19)

Study Notes & Weekly Highlights